Carmichael
Americana on the move

Carmichael is like a box of candy.
You never know what you'll get...

A photographic essay
by Susan Maxwell Skinner

Photographed, written and published in Carmichael, California

Carmichael - Americana on the move

I've been photographing Carmichael for years. Raised in a New Zealand village that vanished into suburbia, I felt someone should document my adopted Carmichael's eccentricities while they still existed.

I soon knew the project was not just about Carmichael. My community exemplifies thousands of towns that cling — even as cities consume them — to rural identities. Nowadays, mansions rise in architectural splendor beside workers' cottages. In this book, contemporary is contrasted with vintage. Not just by buildings; also by society. My pictures don't criticize; they fondly record.

My snaps catalogue more than Carmichael's charm. This study also observes the changing face of Americana. A 1910 water tower salutes pioneer hardship. Waving a toy at fighter jets, a child catapults the American dream into the future. I also offer vignettes of sidewalk kisses and teenage fantasies. I know love is an eternal dream for all generations, all races.

You will note my obeisance to Norman Rockwell. Well, this scion of Americana seems to have painted Carmichael in sentimental hues. Indeed,

Patriotism on the move. Jodette's belly dancers grace the July 4 parade. More folkloric pictures, page 38.

despite the innovations of the 21st Century, our Sacramento County *Mayberry* remains as unhip as Andy Griffiths' hometown. People who grew up here recall halcyon days: riding horseback in the famous July 4 parade; having the revered naturalist Effie Yeaw teach Sunday school.

Returning to raise kids, former Carmichaelites find paradise not lost, but changed.

Belly dancers writhe in the Independence Day parade. An Indian family owns a mansion Governor Ronald Reagan built. There are temples for every faith. A 1920s community slogan bragged "there are no strangers in Carmichael." I contend that America is great because towns like Carmichael are microcosms of a warm-hearted nation, irrevocably under the God of choice.

Norman Rockwell said: "Without knowing too much about it, I (*showed*) the America I observed, to others who might not have noticed." Similarly, I hope to record the essential small American town for those who don't always stop and smell the roses. I also ask you to treasure your own *Mayberry**. It will never be the same again.

Oh, and yes, I love this place.

Susan Maxwell Skinner

*A classic 1960's TV comedy, "The Andy Griffith Show" was set in the fictional town of Mayberry.

Photojournalist Susan Maxwell Skinner came to Carmichael after a New Zealand and English career. She married bandleader John Skinner, served as president of the Carmichael Chamber of Commerce and has long contributed to local newspapers.

For more about Susan's books, see inside back cover.

Who's chicken, ass? Rustic Carmichael offers a whimsical snap for the photojournalist. For more animal tricks, see page 74.

This entire photographics essay was shot with an Olympus E300 digital camera.

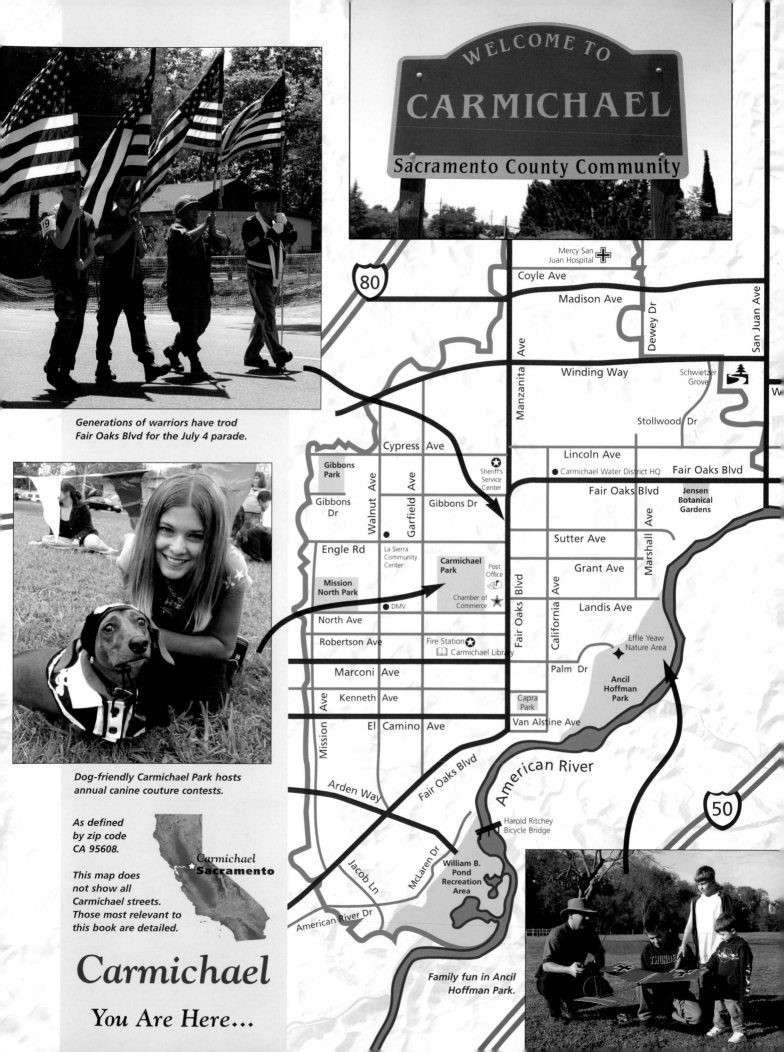

Generations of warriors have trod Fair Oaks Blvd for the July 4 parade.

Dog-friendly Carmichael Park hosts annual canine couture contests.

As defined by zip code CA 95608.

This map does not show all Carmichael streets. Those most relevant to this book are detailed.

Carmichael
Sacramento

Carmichael

You Are Here...

Family fun in Ancil Hoffman Park.

WELCOME TO **CARMICHAEL** Sacramento County Community

Mercy San Juan Hospital
Coyle Ave
Madison Ave
Winding Way
Stollwood Dr
Manzanita Ave
Dewey Dr
San Juan Ave
Schwietzer Grove

Cypress Ave
Gibbons Park
Gibbons Dr
Walnut Ave
Garfield Ave
Gibbons Dr
Sheriff's Service Center
Lincoln Ave
Carmichael Water District HQ
Fair Oaks Blvd
Fair Oaks Blvd
Jensen Botanical Gardens

Engle Rd
La Sierra Community Center
Carmichael Park
Post Office
Sutter Ave
Marshall Ave

Mission North Park
DMV
Chamber of Commerce
Grant Ave
California Ave

North Ave
Landis Ave
Effie Yeaw Nature Area

Robertson Ave
Fire Station
Carmichael Library
Fair Oaks Blvd
Palm Dr
Ancil Hoffman Park

Marconi Ave
Mission Ave
Kenneth Ave
Capra Park
Van Alstine Ave

El Camino Ave
American River

Arden Way
Fair Oaks Blvd
Harold Ritchey Bicycle Bridge

Jacob Ln
McLaren Dr
William B. Pond Recreation Area

American River Dr

A River Runs By Us

Fed by High Sierra snow, the American River's path has shaped Californian geography and history since before the last Ice Ages. Nisenan riverside communities thrived here for millennia. But by the 1830s, Mexican officials called the artery "El Rio de Los Americanos," for the many American trappers then haunting its banks.

Later, argonauts panned fortunes from its riverbeds. Today, river water that provided pioneer Carmichael farmers with the basis for commercial agriculture refreshes many Northern California cities.

Awed by rapids and riverside wilderness, the 19th century explorer Jedediah Smith spoke of the valley's "Wild River." Following its course, an American River Parkway – partly wilderness – today remains sanctuary for about 200 species of birds and animals. The river's wildness still delights those who pause to appreciate its many beauty spots.

Desperately seeking salmon. A "Buck" lurks in gravelly river shallows near Ancil Hoffman Park. The November-December salmon run has lured fishermen since prehistoric times.

An autumn vista - including the San Juan Rapids - is framed by lantana bushes. A turkey vulture soars where eagles dare.

On a clear day.
A winter bluff visit leads the eye to the High Sierras.

An aerial view of the American River as it meanders by Carmichael. The Harold Ritchey Bicycle Bridge links Goethe and William B. Pond recreation areas.

Aerial view made possible by 111th Aerial Photography Squadron.

Huckleberry friends. Though riverboats plied the American River during the 19th Century, modern traffic is mostly recreational. Rafting is a summer diversion for Carmichael teenagers, braving rapids near William B. Pond Park.

A spectacular sunset at the Harrington Way river access.

4000-plus Years of Community

Ancestors of the Nisenan Maidu formed Carmichael's first communities. For thousands of summers, bluff-dwelling villagers made temporary settlements on the American River floodplain.

Modern Nisenan (above), don traditional garments for annual festivities at the Effie Yeaw Nature Center. See more, page 44.

Carmichael was a wilderness when Hudson Bay Company trappers headed south from the Columbia River area. Some brought wives or married native women. Left: former Carmichael Parks and Recreation head Ron Cuppy reenacts the frontier life. His pioneer partner is Debra Henningsen.

Carmichael straddles parts of the old San Juan and Del Paso Spanish land grants. Built on Rancho Del Paso in the 1850s, Carmichael's oldest building (left), is also the oldest home in Sacramento. The homestead was center of a 44,000-acre thoroughbred stud. For more on this house, see page 25.

Carmichael's Deterding clan was established by pioneers Charles and Mary Deterding. From the early 1900s, they farmed hundreds of riverside acres. Pillars of the early community, the couple eased the way for families who settled real estate developer Daniel Carmichael's colony after 1909.

Right: Deterding descendants on the former family farm, now a park named for early County Supervisor Ancil Hoffman.

A 1930's Deterding family home (below) is now a Carmichael landmark.

Daniel Carmichael's first 2000-acre colony promised settlers success through orange groves (bottom left). But many farmers had to dynamite hardpan soil to plant trees.

Although founder Carmichael wanted the main street (Fair Oaks Blvd) named for him, the area's tallest apartment block (below), now dignifies the only road bearing Carmichael's name.

9

On the Hoof

In the early 1900s, Daniel Carmichael sold off ten-acre parcels that included parts of the former San Juan and later, Del Paso Mexican land grants. His second colony had previously housed the biggest horse stud in the world, Rancho del Paso. Fittingly, chunks of Carmichael remain equestrian to the fetlock.

Thanks a latte! A Carmichael teen (above), combines a love for all things equestrian and caffeinated.

Beside California Ave, horse trainer Gena Wasley (above), takes thoroughbred Tucker for a daily constitutional.

A garden statue (above), marks a former horse property.

Left: fourth-generation horse rancher Colleen Dennison gives Arab thoroughbreds Echo and D'Artagnon a peek through the family gate.

Carriage driving champions Carolee and Steve Smith (above), tool an antique "Victorian" along Marshall Ave. Carolee runs a bespoke harness business from the family home.

Galen Grow (left), leads thoroughbred Geronimo on an autumn stroll. Grow's family has owned the Hughes Ranch since 1935.

Foaling around. Newly born colt Skylar (below), pauses for a spring break on a family horse property off Garfield Ave. His dam is palomino Raleighhanna.

Toon Town Americana

What some Carmichael establishments - and residents - lack in sophistication, they make up in character. Disney-bright stores dot the central area. Local characters are colorful, too...

"Feed for any critter" is merchandize offered by the Western Feed Store (left), Don Way. Founded in 1950, the business recalls a period when many Carmichael merchants adopted western themes. Current owner is Matt Boyer (with horse).

Above: in cartoon-inspired duds, halloweenies take to the streets.

Center: Carmichael Home Appliances 1935 building previously served as a garage, theater and plumbing store. 1960 Cadillac courtesy Larry Bunfill.

Left: for 50 years, Frank and Dolores Impinna ran an accordion and dance studio in their pink Fair Oaks Blvd premises. At the height of Lawrence Welk fame, they furnished multiple accordion bands per night. Three years after Frank's death in 2002, Dolores sold out.

Above: a 1945 Quonset hut houses the Ace Muffler store. Owner Mark Rankin (right), inspects Bob McDonald's 1957 Bel Air.

Popeye's palace. The Tugboat Fish and Chip shop's cartoon-style façade (left), nets diners on Fair Oaks Blvd.

Below: on Landis Ave, 2001 Corvette owner Dan Perry compares his custom paint job to that of neighbor Bob Hopkins' 1930 Model A.

Below: assistant manager at Beverly's Craft Store, Jan Strickland founded the Bev's Angels organization. Her volunteers make quilts and gifts for needy children. Strickland also doubles as Mrs Easter Bunny and Mrs Santa Claus for store festivities.

Sugar and Spice. Olivia's Doll House hosts tea parties for little girls. Right: a younger brother endures "feminization" at his sister's birthday.

A monument to fairytales, the Fair Oaks Blvd business even crowns its company car (left), with a tiara.

14

Nifty, Thrifty Recycling Carmichael

Inhabiting the recycling capital of Sacramento may not be the ambition for all Carmichaelites. But with antique, thrift or consignment stores in many commercial blocks, the area's attraction for budget-minded shoppers cannot be denied.

Second-hand roses. Thrift shops offer haute couture for the Carmichael-based retro singing group, Sister Swing. In vintage performance duds, (right), the songstresses sift for bargains at WEAVE. The outlet was voted Best Thrift Store by Sacramento Magazine readers.

Below: objets d'art and d'artifice form an intriguing pyramid at Bad Kitty Antiques.

Below right: in the Magnolia Antiques emporium, English-born dealer Susan Powers finds vintage crockery just her cup of tea.

French-born vendeuse Maryse Normand named her Marconi Ave consignment business (above), after the building's paint job. "I did not know the expression 'tickled pink' then," she recalls, "but it was parfait!" Her 1953 building previously sold Western wear. 1956 Cadillac Seville courtesy Elmer Bunfill.

Left and below: weekend observances of an all-American ritual: The Yard Sale.

GARAGE SALE

Carmichael Landmarks and Claims to Fame...

Carmichael has no Big Ben, nor even a town hall. But some local landmarks are as familiar as Carmichaelites' own back yards.

Below: this early 1940's home belonged to Carmichael's second most revered matriarch, Effie Yeaw. The naturalist gave her name to a wildlife reserve in Ancil Hoffman Park. The current owner shares Yeaw's fondness for wildflowers.

In the early 1920s, pioneer Carmichael matriarch Mary Deterding planted the road to her farmstead with palms. This landmark route (above), became stately Palm Drive.

Water everywhere. Disused but still functional, a 1956 water tower keeps sentinel in Ancil Hoffman Park. 2006 winter floods half submerged the landmark, which remains the property of the Carmichael Water District.

Art imitating art. Muralist Hugh Gorman's 100ft Carmichael Park mural earned a 2003 award for depicting area history. Gorman (left), applauds chalk work by Carmichael sisters Lexi and Livi. "Art should inspire other artists," says the painter.

Below: established in 1923, Carmichael Presbyterian Church has the oldest local congregation. Parishioners built the smaller adobe chapel during WW2. A larger sanctuary building and bell tower were added in the 1950s. See aerial view, page 21.

With the shovel (right), California Governor Ronald Reagan broke ground for a home on California Ave in 1974. View the completed mansion, page 32.

Top: bridge over flowing water. Linking William B. Pond and Goethe Parks, the Harold Ritchey Bicycle Bridge (above), is a graceful conduit for hikers and cyclists on the American River Bike Trail.

Olympian Mark Spitz trained in Arden Hills Country Club's azure pools (above).

The club spa (right), was voted Best Day Spa by Sacramento Magazine readers.

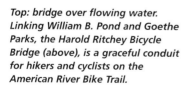

Behind the same landmark cypress border is a secluded seven-acre sanctuary. Above: Swami Prapannananda selects flowers for the Vedanta Society altar. Founded in 1950, the monastery and temple promotes study of ancient Indian spiritualism.

Tale of Two Towers

Water tank towers were once common to all rural towns. Two that remain in Carmichael bear testimony to pioneer endeavor.

Norwegian immigrant Paul Osterli built his tank house in 1911 beside the Osterli farmhouse near Mission Ave. Soon after he married the Osterli homestead burned down. During rebuilding, the newlyweds and an infant son lived in the narrow tower, left.

Right: built in the 1920s near Cypress Ave, this persimmon-framed tank tower was originally part of a Carmichael homestead. Surrounding area farms produced fruit, walnuts and olives. Turkeys were also bred in huge numbers

From a Distance

Above: a November evening colors Marconi Ave. Glowing like an ivory chess piece, the Carmichael Presbyterian Church tower gives the landscape a touch of New England.

Left: palms that pioneer Mary Deterding planted in the 1920s still define Palm Dr. Carmichael revered naturalist Effie Yeaw lived in the house lower left. See page 17 for a close-up.

City lights. As the crow flies, the Californian capital city of Sacramento (above), is about ten miles away. A telephoto lens brings it closer. The Coastal Range provides a muted backdrop.

Bird's-eye view. From 120ft up, Sacramento Metropolitan Fire Department engineer Beau Perry (center above), gets a unique perspective on Carmichael's main street.

Once voted Sacramento's "ugliest street," Fair Oaks Blvd (right), is somewhat enhanced by a fall sunset.

Anglers' Paradise

From steelhead trout to bass, shad and salmon, Carmichael anglers rejoice in a full fishing calendar. The fall salmon run is irresistable to fishermen (above and below), from all over Northern California.

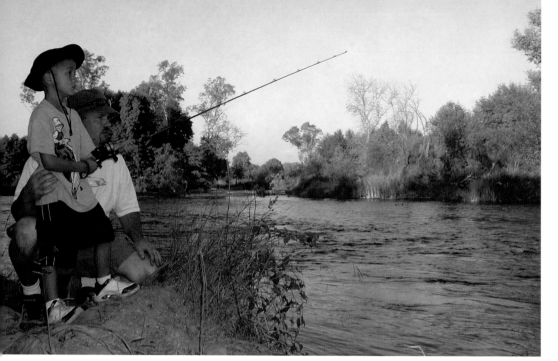

In Norman Rockwell tradition (left), a Carmichael dad teaches his son the noble art of casting.

Another angler (right), is assured of a REALLY big dinner.

Below: a moonlit evening at the Harrington Ave river access rewards anglers with dangling shad by the score.

After spawning (below right), salmon soon die and become food for other river creatures.

Sacramento's Oldest House, Carmichael

Hidden on a Carmichael side street, this 5000 sq ft home and two-acre garden is all that remains of Rancho Del Paso, the final Spanish land grant. This 44,000-acre parcel stretched to Rio Linda and was granted to Eliah Grimes in 1844. San Franciscan James Ben Ali Haggin later acquired the property. By the 1860s, Haggin's ranch was the world-famous horse stud that produced Kentucky Derby winner Ben Ali. According to utility records, the 1857 farmhouse is the oldest home in Sacramento.

Complete with original marble fireplace (below), the wedding-cake Victorian is now lovingly preserved by the Niello family.

Vintage Carmichael

Recalling the community's turn-of-the century founding, scores of vintage homes line Carmichael's older streets. While many have been preserved, rising property values means the more humble cottages are vanishing fast. Others, with greater historical provence, are carefully preserved.

Right: Nancy and Allan Davis maintain this sprawling circa-1910 ranch house, completely built from Carmichael adobe brick.

Below: Canadian-born brothers Jim and Drew Dickson were popular Carmichael bricklayers from 1920 onwards. Jim's California Ave home is one of many lasting memorials to the family trade.

This 1914 cottage's mullioned windows (right), were salvaged from an ancient English Tudor building.

This all-redwood 1908 house (above), was originally
the homestead for a citrus orchard.

Sara Lott kept a wall of books in this Landis Ave house
(above). During the 1920s, her collection served local families
as Carmichael's first lending library.

Sacramento Bee newspaper owner C.K. McClatchy enjoyed this
modest 1918 lodge (above) for vacations and, in declining health,
ran the newspaper from the refuge during his final years.
The print legend died here in 1936.

Above: since 1926, four generations of the Pefley
family have lived in this Palm Dr house.

Building in 1934, the first owner of this
English-style cottage utilized available materials.
The inner staircase is made from railroad ties.

Above right: this 1936 home commands a view of the American River.

The Fred Dickson family home (above left), is barely changed since 1917, when the original owner established a peach orchard beside Palm Dr.

Right: a German family built this Tudor-style home on Fair Oaks Blvd in 1917. The current owners still rejoice in 1.5 immaculate acres of garden.

This charming cottage was built in 1936 and in 2006 was still housing a member of its original family.

Below right: this home's acerage was subdivided in the 1930s from a Sutter Ave walnut orchard.

Below: built after 1906, this ranch house is thought to contain bricks salvaged from San Francisco earthquake rubble.

In the 1950s, a convent and religious retreat was established beside Fair Oaks Blvd and run by Cenacle nuns. The Sacramento Catholic Diocese later sold the property. Developer Danny Benvenuti subdivided the land and the prestigious Cenacle neighborhood rose in the place of the old retreat. All that remains of the former sanctuary is the marble figure above, secluded in a private garden. The statue, poignantly, is of Saint Anthony - patron of lost causes.

Left: famed Carmichael mason Drew Dickson slavishly modeled his stone cottage after a French farmhouse, where he was billeted during WWI. One of the prettiest homes in Carmichael, its care has been a labor of love for successive owners.

Top: this graceful 1940s neo-Georgian was the homestead on a gentleman farmer's Retreat Dr. acres. Solidly built of old growth redwood, the villa was restored by the Buck family.

Above: this 1921 house was modernized during the 1950s. In the 1970s, the Gregory family began the long process of returning their villa to Depression-era simplicity.

Though built yards inside neighboring Fair Oaks, the first owners of this 1876 home influenced Carmichael's earliest agriculture. Harold Dewey farmed 160 acres around his homestead and leased vast tracts of the San Juan grant. His orchards sprawled over what is now Carmichael Park. Six generations of his descendants, including the present occupants, were reared in the Dewey farmhouse. The pillared verandah was added in 1911.

In with the New

An incongruous hotchpotch of old and new – affluent and humble – typifies Carmichael's 17 square miles. Architect-designed mansions are commonly yards from wooden cottages.

Left: junior excavators get to work on a former Fair Oaks Blvd farm, earmarked for a 14-home 2006 subdivision.

Center and above: this 1997 Euro-eclectic mansion dominates almost two acres overlooking the American River.

The 1980s "pole house," near California Ave (left), was designed to straddle a valley carved by Carmichael Creek. After storms, says the owner, "the water below us just boils."

Above: with peerless river views, this one-level home was finished in 2003. Clad entirely in custom-cut Italian marble, its 4,200 sq ft living area presesnts a minimalist facade (right), from the street.

Below: inside and out, Asian simplicity triumphs in this 2002 design. Built to resemble a village, the Getz-Mahony home features many courtyards and an artist's studio.

Welcome back! After closing shop for a year during a $6.8 million reconstruction, Carmichael Library opened in fall of 2006. Built on a former olive grove, the 21,000 sq ft facility is the busiest of all Sacramento County libraries. Returning Pat Mahony's "The Olive Tree" to pride of place are (left), artist Mahony, Branch Supervisor Jill Stockinger, California Arts Council Director (former County Supervisor) Muriel Johnson and project manager Lois Ross.

Left: the Beutler family's own swan lake is a classical touch for a minimalist 2000 home. A spiral staircase (below), was crafted to echo ancient oaks in the five-acre garden. The mansion's living room, above, blends modern and primitive styles.

Left: challenged to incorporate a state-of-the-art utility building into a placid residential street, the Carmichael Water District disguised its 22,000 sq ft purification plant as a large house. Oversized bricks complete the trompe l'oeil on Bajamont Way. Staffers are (left), Greg Stinson, Mark McClintock and manager Steve Nugent.

A cul-de-sac suprises with olde English charm. Anglophile Gayle Stimack began planning her dream home as a child. During its construction in 1991, the professional designer and husband Jay adzed dozens of Tudor-style beams by hand.

Above: a bronze boar brings a touch of Florence to a massive villa near Ancil Hoffman Park. Rebuilt in the 1970s, its interior (right and far right), continues the Stephens' family's Renaissance theme.

Home Sweet Mansion

In 1974, California Governor Ronald Reagan began building a home on California Ave. He intended for succeeding governors to occupy what was planned as the Casa de los Gobernadores (Governor's Mansion). After the Reagans moved to the White House, the property fell into private hands. In 2004 it was bought by Dr Janek Mehtani. Now US, California and Indian flags fly over the sprawling compound where Mehtani, wife Nalini and an extended family co-exist with Rupert, the mansion's longtime resident peacock.

You Gotta Have Faith

Carmichael's churchgoing founders were mainly Protestant. The following century has seen many additions to area religion.

Above: Father Louis Alessio conducts services in Latin at St Michael's Roman Catholic Church.

Left: hot from Utah, missionaries pedal from the Garfield Ave L.D.S. Stake.

Below: a Hindu woman observes the festival of Diwali in her home.

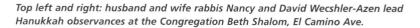

Top left and right: husband and wife rabbis Nancy and David Wecshler-Azen lead Hanukkah observances at the Congregation Beth Shalom, El Camino Ave.

Above: the Slavic Pentecostals now worship in the prim California Ave building that once housed a ladies' bridge club. Pastor (top right), is Vladimir Gavirlov.

As it has since the 1920s, the Carmichael Presbyterian Church choir (right), makes a joyful noise.

Below: Vietnamese beautician Kim Le prays to Buddha in Rosie's Hair and Nail Salon.

Flirtation, Love and Marriage is in the Air...

Right: on cigarette break, waiters from long-established Carmichael restaurant Café Capri applaud a fresh diversion–in Capri pants, yet.

April showers bring May flowers. Sweethearts (below), share a not-quite private proposal at the Brothers Papadopoulos florist shop. Her answer? Guess.

Eighteen wheels and a dozen roses. Greeting wife Debbie after a drive from Texas, trucker Gary Lobaugh repeats the sentiments of a classic country song. Their California Ave digs is dwarfed by the couple's 2005 Peterbuilt.

Left: father marries daughter. American River Community Church Pastor Richard Reimer gives an ecstatic blessing to daughter Adelle and her new husband, Todd Plain.

Television meteorologist Tom Loffman pledges his troth–rain or shine–to bride Debbie (below), at the Arden Hills Country Club.

Ever the bridesmaid. Fitting a wedding gown at Euro Bridal, bride and vendeuse are oblivious to a bridesmaid's dreams. The junior attendants find the whole flower girl gig a huge joke.

Above: ever and ever, amen. Carmichaelites Jack and Jill Flint were still holding hands on their 60th wedding anniversary. Their secret? "Do what ever you want," said 95-year-old Jack. "Just be sure to do it together…"

Don't forget folks, that's what you get folks…Carmichael parents Gen and Conor McNulty find life will never be the same after the birth of their quads. The mom is a great, great grandaughter of Carmichael's founders, Charles and Mary Deterding.

Secret tea garden. Classical Japanese music instructor, Dr Eiko Bernier, plucks a melody from her antique shamisen in a Carmichael hideaway.

Folkloric Vignettes of the World

As a microcosm of the American nation, Carmichael has been enriched by an influx of international culture since its founding days.

Above: entertainers stay on the ball at Carmichael's annual Founders Day festival.

Above: Bollywood dreams. Screen romance is not just a Western addiction; Indian teens and moms enjoy a spicy Hollywood ending – Bombay-style – at the Sher E Punjab restaurant.

Below: mitzvah mom Jennifer Goldwyn holds on for dear life during son Aaron's coming of age party at Arden Hills Country Club.

Above: Balkan beauties display embroidered finery for an annual Romanian festival at Carmichael Park.

Above: Ukrainian-born Lydia Tsarenko is one of many immigrant gardeners who produce bounties from a community garden loaned by the San Juan School District.

Above: food server at El Papagaya Restaurant, Senora Leticia dresses to emphasize her striking likeness to Mexican heroine Frida Kahlo.

In garments crafted from eagle and flicker feathers, Native Americans dance at the Effie Yeaw Nature Center. The fall Maidu Day festival (below), celebrates the culture of Carmichael's earliest communities.

Country Roads

Ten miles from the bustling California Capital, some Carmichael roadsides have yet to curb their rusticity.

Left, with kids grown and flown, a Carmichael mom enjoys a nostalgic tree-house moment.

Below: morning glory festoons a Landis Ave gate.

Before retiring at the age of 82, "Zinnia Lady" Dorothy Houpt (above), sold the produce of her California Ave flower beds every summer.

Who will buy? Carmichael's "Egg Lady" Debbie Conover (above left), offers her wares on Landis Ave. Homegrown eggs, she says, taste better because her free-range hens (above), are happier and healthier.

Some Carmichael property boundaries (left) do not exactly fence anyone in.

Below left: Calfornia Ave's "Blue Swing Lady" decorates "to cheer people when they drive past my house."

Below right: the fall persimmon harvest provides pocket money for some senior entrepreneurs.

Eager beaver. Cruising in slow backwaters near Jacob Ave, beaver kits gnaw on willow and other riverside vegetation. Their parents make dens in nearby banks.

On the Wilder Side

Carmichael's proximity to the American River Parkway makes for many close encounters of the animal kind.

Left: an oak tree at the Effie Yeaw Nature Preserve shelters a raccoon baby. (Picture by Jim McMurtry).

Right: a coyote hunts at dawn in the William B. Pond Park. The feral dogs forage in many areas of the American River Parkway and often venture into Carmichael streets.

O, possum! Staff at the Effie Yeaw Nature Center cared for Opal (above), an abandoned marsupial with a balance problem. The orphan became a star to visiting children and was later returned to the wild.

Deer, Here and Everywhere

Roaming uphill from the American River Parkway, deer are home on the free-range in much of Carmichael.

Top left: at the Effie Yeaw Nature Preserve, black tailed deer twins show markings that allow new-borns to blend with the dappled light of bush thickets.

Three-legged buck "Tripod" (above), has haunted the Effie Yeaw Nature Preserve for years.

Right: antlers at dawn. Rutting bucks battle to win does.

A California Ave resident takes pride the ultimate garden accessory: a private deer herd. His does (above), present a new generation of fawns every spring.

Left center: fawns awake on the river flood plain.

Below: golf wars. Wooing his harem, a dominant buck delays play at Ancil Hoffman Golf Course.

Feathered Friends

The sanctuary of the American River Parkway and mature Carmichael gardens provide a bird watcher's paradise.

Above: an egret anticipates lunch in Ancil Hoffman Park.

Top center: Canada geese make a perfect dawn landing.

Right: a swan and duck make an odd couple at William B. Pond Park.

Below, the bane of many Carmichael gardeners, wild turkeys indulge a December courtship

Above right: girl Talk. Two hens ignore their husband as the plumed California quail stands sentry over his little flock.

Right: with the endurance of Methuselah, a great blue heron awaits breakfast at William B. Pond Park. Below: the bird presents an awesome silhouette in flight.

51

Golden Pond. A five-acre garden
(above), glows like Carmichael's
own Narnia.

*Left: after a wet 2005 spring, a
massive crop of sunflowers
volunteered in Jack and Jerri
Pefley's Palm Dr. vineyard. Said
Jack of his green stalks: "We don't
know where they came from.
We never planted them."*

How Does Your Garden Grow?

Below: the Carmichael Water District Office (Fair Oaks Blvd), shows the possibilities of drought-tolerant gardening. Even in heat waves, plants thrive on minimal watering.

A garden scarecrow (below left), dons patriotic garb for July 4.

Below: crape myrtle groves are ubiquitous Carmichael summer color spots.

Above: planted in the 1950s, cacti thrive in a vintage garden.

Volunteer gardeners (above), tend a towering zinnia border in the Carmichael Community Garden.

Below: boots are made for working. But even the most industrious California Ave gardener deserves a break.

A rose arbor (above), offers a spectacular welcome.

Left: a creek bisects a property settled in the 1800s.

Below: a formal avenue divides this secluded Mediterranean-style garden near Landis Ave.

Humming birds (above left), feed near Sutter Ave.

Above: on land loaned by the Parks and Recreation District, the Carmichael Community Garden (Sutter Ave), is divided into 60 rented allotments. The garden is a haven for the green-fingered.

Left: tulips bloom in the botanical gardens planted in the 1950s by Charles C. Jensen. The park is on Fair Oaks Blvd.

Below center: after felling a massive oak on Oak Ave, a winter storm revealed a fairytale folly.

Left and above: the Vedanta Society's gardens (Mission Ave), proudly boast a spectacular spring display and one of very few lotus ponds in California. The exotic water flowers bloom in June and July.

Great racer. As halfway point in the California Internatinal Marathon, Carmichael annually garners world attention. In dawning light, 2005 winner, Russian Sergey Fedotov thunders past Carmichael's central park.

Below: by mid morning, marathoners crowd Fair Oaks Blvd.

Good Sports...

On the road and in the water; in studios and parks, Carmichael hosts many sporting events. Some are the focus of world notice; others are simply small town traditions.

Above: tournaments bring disk golf players to the Schweitzer Grove Nature Area, AKA "Little Africa", near Stollwood Dr. Played with Frisbee-like disks, the lesser-known sport follows basic rules of golf. The Carmichael Parks and Recreation District administers the course and nature reserve.

Right: a tournament contestant throws an upshot.

On the American River Bike Trail, a husband and wife athletic team mark the parting of the ways...

Petit Prix. In true American tradition, Cub Scouts contest an annual "pinewood derby" at the Carmichael Presbyterian Church. Whittled from pine blocks, cars compete in heats lasting under four seconds!

The kayak portion of Eppie's Great Race clogs the American River each July. The world's oldest triathlon has passed under Carmichael's river bluffs since 1974. The event fundraises for therapeutic recreation services.

League of their own. Nationally ranked, the Yard Sharks girls' softball team (above), has pitched fast balls at Carmichael Park since 1992. Coach to the teenagers is Carmichael businessman Joe Price.

Right: Strike! The Californian Women's Bowling Association staged a state-wide tournament at Carmichael's Crestview lanes in 2006

Celebrity Sightings

Sacramento television legend Stan Atkinson (right), learned to play golf at Carmichael's Ancil Hoffman Park Golf Course. The big-hearted news anchor now volunteers for the First Tee of Greater Sacramento, a non-profit that teaches children the skills and etiquette of golf.

Anchors ahoy! Morning television hosts Marianne McClary (left), and Tina Macuha catch up on industry gossip over breakfast at the Waffle Barn. Both live in Carmichael. Their date is veteran television meteorologist Tom Loffman. Server is Shyla Russ.

Running for California Attorney general in 2006, Oakland Mayor Jerry Brown (left), campaigned at the former Governor's Mansion in Carmichael. Matching wits with Brown was Indian community leader Didar Bains.

Below: super-swimmer Debbie Meyer got her picture on Wheaties boxes after winning three gold medals at the 1968 Olympics. She now teaches at her own Carmichael swim school.

Below: man with a horn. Leader of one of the most popular big bands in Northern California, John Skinner jams with a junior fan. A Carmichael resident and mentor to young musicians, Skinner has performed in Carmichael Park concerts since the 1970s.

Movers and Shakers...

A vociferous champion of Carmichael interests, the Carmichael Chamber of Commerce evolved from the 1913 Carmichael Colony Improvement Club, whose members pledged to "promote harmony and social welfare." With similar motives, the existing Chamber was formed in 1948.

A Chamber staple was the Miss Carmichael Pageant. Twin sisters Sheryl Ellis and Sharon Buckenmeyer won 1994 and 1997 tiaras. After their marriages, both sisters took turns as Mrs California. Sheryl (seated left), has introduced her daughters to junior pageants.

Right: in 2002, a trail-blazing Youth Ambassador program replaced beauty contests. Selected for community service, male and female teen volunteers now learn the ropes of local administration. Ambassadors have included (from left), Aubrey Winn, Kiersten Vance, Hayley Andersen, Michelle Rajender, Casey Hoehn and Mary McCune.

Hail the chiefs. Breaking bread at Steve's Place Pizza Restaurant, 15 former presidents of the Carmichael Chamber of Commerce (below), enjoy their last reunion supper. Four-times president Bonnie Berns (center) cradles a sepia snap of Danny Carmichael.

Living Carmichael Chamber of Commerce presidents include (seated from left): Kathy Plumb, Mark Hart, Don McIntyre, Colleen Todd, Bruce Mizer, Bonnie Berns, Kevin Brennan, Gary R. Anderson, Cindy Templeton, Major Nilson, and Lyle Jewel. Back Row: Roni Sahota (restaurant franchisee), Jan Bass Otto (Executive Vice President), Barry Smith, Gary Hursh, Ross Davidson, Susan Maxwell Skinner and franchise creator Steve Wilkinson.

Elect me, elect my dog. County Supervisor Susan Peters (above with terrier Bryn), is a popular face at the annual dog show in Carmichael Park.

Below: State Senator (Grandpa) Dave Cox treats his grandkids to dessert at Coldstone Creamery.

Above: Congressman Dan Lungren goes one-on-300 with Carmichael constituents. The La Sierra Community Center (Engle Ave), often serves as Carmichael town hall.

State Senator Deborah Ortiz (right), long represented a small slice of Carmichael, where she back-peddled from politics during dawn bike rides on the American River Parkway.

Route 95608. Fifth District Assemblyman Roger Niello (below right), cruises Fair Oaks Blvd in a vintage Buick. Driver is his auto dealer brother, Carmichael resident Rick Niello.

Back to School...

San Juan Elementary School started in 1880, near present-day Winding Way. In 1917, Carmichael founder Daniel Carmichael offered 10 acres on Sutter Ave – if the school would move and change its name. It did. By 2006, the roll numbered 510. Serving Carmichael, the San Juan School District now administers 76 schools.

Above, Principal Tambria Swift welcomes kids from a 1917 San Juan School District bus.

Theresa Hollenbeck (standing left), is an award-winning San Juan District science teacher at Winston Churchill Middle School. Boning up on comparative anatomy with seventh graders is skeletal classroom mascot, George.

Jesuit High's Junior and Varstiy Cross Country team hares across hallowed turf on Jacob Lane. The Catholic boys school opened in 1963. Many of its sports teams have been nationally ranked. "Play hard, pray hard," is a school motto.

Nuts about you. Co-directors of Schweitzer Elementary theatricals, Denise Josephson and Laurie Struckmeyer (above), were on squirrel alert during a production of Roald Dahl's "Charlie and the Chocolate Factory." The school annually stages junior extravaganzas in its own theater.

Garfield Elementary pupils (below), study pond life with famed Carmichael nature mentor, Earl "Ranger Jack" Koobs. The school is custodian to a five-acre wilderness nature reserve.

Pioneer Mary Deterding gave her name to a school. Deterding Elementary's 50th jubilee celebrations (right), welcomed Carmichael Honorary Mayor Donna Deterding - a former student and Deterding descendant - back to school. In spectacles is Principal Donna Kentfield.

Go Cougars! Del Campo High cheerleaders (below), inspire the school basketball team to greater effort. Though located yards inside neighboring Fair Oaks, the Dewey Ave school serves as a public high school for Carmichael teens.

Patriotic Carmichael

July 4 fervor and fireworks do not define Carmichael patriotism. The community parades red white and blue Americana 365 days of the year.

The Sons of the American Revolution organization (below), sports colonial garb to reenact War of Independence scenarios. Their young fifer girl is romantically named Madison.

Right: veterans of the Iraq conflict, Air Force Captain Kathryn and Major Christian Seher add a patriotic flavor to their 2005 wedding. Model T courtesy of Frank Z'berg.

Bottom right: soldier's homecoming. US Army Specialist Adam Brown returns to Carmichael after ten months in Iraq, where his 21st birthday came and went. California Ave traffic presents the colors as parents Pat and Pastor William Brown (Carmichael Baptist Church) rejoice in a moment of thanksgiving.

Above: at restaurant Rey Azteca, artist Pablo's outdoor mural celebrates Hispanic contributions to American liberty

Band of brothers. Siblings Tommy and Sammy (left), march in the July 4 parade. Organized by the Carmichael Elks, the parade marshalls over 2000 participants.

Below: Del Campo High School Air Force Junior ROTC cadets spruce up before presenting colors at a San Juan School District meeting. Their instructor is Col. Earl Farney.

Above: veterans of over 60 years of wars honor the fallen at the Carmichael Vietnam War Memorial. Bearing 17 names, the memorial plaque (right), shows La Sierra High School's heavy Vietnam losses.

VIETNAM

ROBERT D. ANDERSON   RALPH GUARIENTI
MARK W. BURCHARD   LARRY H. MORFORD
ROBERT S. BYRNES   THOMAS C. PIGG
JERRY COWSERT   RANDALL B. RAINVILLE
KENNETH R. ESCOTT   KIM RICHINS
GARY R. FIELD   JEFFERY THARALDSON
HERBERT FRENZELL   ROBERT A. WILLIS
FRANK THORNBURG

Dear Boys we will never forget your Sacrifice xx

Left: top gun. As the famed US Navy Blue Angels fighter jets soar above Ancil Hoffman Park, a young man makes a career choice.

VETERAN'S MEMORIAL

Indivisible under God, Veterans of Foreign Wars (Post 2324) pledge allegiance at their monthly meeting in Carmichael. Mostly octogenarians, dwindling WW2 survivors are reinforced by veterans from Korean and Vietnam Wars. Their ranks are boosted here by Ladies Auxiliary members.

In the Name of the Law...

The Sacramento Sheriff's Department and the California Highway Patrol are respected and compassionate presences in Carmichael.

Top cops. Sacramento Sheriffs Lou Blanas and John McGinness honor fallen deputies. Complete with motorcycle honor guard, the 2006 ceremony dedicated a memorial rose garden at the Sheriff's training Academy, River Walk Way.

Enjoying cake and ice cream, the California Highway Patrol marked its 75th anniversary in summer of 2004. From left, celebrating officers were Max Hartley, Rich Andework, Katherina Elson and George McKinley.

Right: by nature, even Carmichael wildlife tries to abide by the law!

The Sacramento Sheriff's Canine Detail works out regularly at the Sheriff's Training facility in Carmichael. Above: Sergeant Raylene Cully leads the detail across the Harold Ritchey Bicycle Bridge.

Right: good cop, bogus cop. Popular Carmichael Sergeant Bob Erikson paid a friendly call to a former Carmichael restaurant whose wait-staff wore mock-cop duds.

Knights of the road. CHP officers (above), allow safe passage to three little maids from the El Rancho Elementary School.

Left: the Northern Area Teen Center provides after-school activities for Carmichael kids. Local Sheriff's officers and Sheriff's volunteers are mentors for the teenagers.

Clever Carmichael Critters...

A more animal-friendly community than Carmichael could scarcely exist.

Above: mini-Schnauzer Cindy's bubble-bursting feat won a "Cutest Trick" prize for mistress Kelli at a Camichael Park dog show.

Elmo and Ernie (right), are two California Ave watchdogs who know their places.

Below: the Hearts and Hooves animal therapy organization brings miniature horses for mutual adoration at the Atrium of Carmichael senior residence.

Above: Old McDonald has a goat-and-hen double act.

TASHA THE DOG!
NO DELIVERIES.

Therapy cat Pecan (above), likes to shop in the Carmichael Incredible Pets store. Mum, Lara, says the 15-pound kitty makes her preferences clear.

Watchdog Tasha (left), has yet to daunt the fainthearted.

Luau Leon (above), is the best dressed cat on Deodar St. His parents admit they need to get a life.

Above right: near California Ave, a fawn beats the birds to a cool drink.

Right: on command, an Australian shepherd in a hound tooth skirt stuns Carmichael Park dog show judges by leaping up from down under.

Far right: enormous but timid watchdog, Irish wolfhound Dominic, just wants someone to open the door that he dwarfs.

Those Who Care...

Carmichael organizations and individuals are quick to lend helping hands – and hearts.

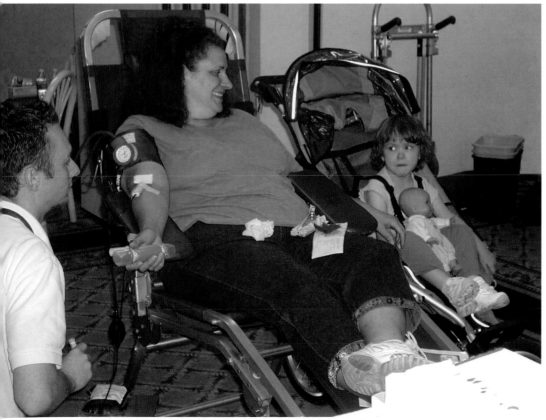

Above: during the annual U.S. Post Office food drive, mail deliverers Shay Campbell (foreground) and Al Schoonover collect groceries for the needy. The food donor is Marie Mustra.

Left: don't hurt Mommy! A blood drive at Mercy San Juan hospital means high anxiety for a Carmichael tot and dolly.

Above: Mad Hatters volunteers knit caps for newborn babies at the Mercy San Juan Hospital, Coyle Ave. Right: Haley, Carmichael's first-born 2006 baby, dozes in her fluffy chapeau. Besotted parents are Tara and Karl Bauman.

Several volunteer groups are dedicated to preserving Carmichael's semi-rural environment. Above: Sandra Dunn, president of the Carmichael Creek Neighborhood Association, leads a clean up of the artery that feeds into the American River.

Santa's little helpers (above), Carmichael kids stuff stockings for underpriviledged children.

Below: bench with a view. The Carmichael Rotary Club furnished benches in Ancil Hoffman Park. Enjoying the riverside seat are Rotarian Stan Roe and his daughter and grandkids.

Owl be seeing you. Retired biologist/ecologist Jack Hiehle (above), is a revered wildlife mentor and leader of nature rambles on the American River Parkway. Octogenarian Hiehle and Effie Yeaw naturalist Denise Booth admire Luna, a popular Nature Center resident.

The energetic Carmichael Kiwanis Club annually hosts a food and wine fundraiser called A Taste of Carmichael. The event (below), showcases local restaurants and merchants. Ruthlessly flogging raffle tickets is 2006 president, Mike Vidalis.

Greenacres is the Place to be...

On California Ave, Anne Marie Usher brings a bouquet to pet heifer Cali.

Above: strange tablemates. A pet pig shares dessert with sheep near Garfield Ave.

Left: tucked away in family acreage, a vineyard shows its spring colors. Michael Patatucci (above), oversees wine production.

Just yards from Fair Oaks Blvd traffic, an apiarist (right), tends family bee hives.

Above: with no fear of Thanksgiving, turkeys gobble happily on Marshall Ave. Their yard-mate is a South American rhea.

Even pet dog Rylee (right), lends a hand with the Greenwood family's winter firewood haul.

Family Business is our Business

While the breakdown of the family unit is nationally lamented, Carmichael clans still push the business on...

Originally from Czechoslovakia, three generations of the Danek family have baked for a living. Their cakes and cookies have been a temptation at the Crestview Shopping Center since the 1970s. Envious window shoppers (right), watch matriarch Becky and son Chris put the icing on the cake.

Above: for half a century, the Warrick family has voluntarily run July 4 parades for the Carmichael Elks. Barnie and Lola Warrick kicked off the patriotic pageant in 1959, roping in their kids. Here parade queen Lola rides with her co-planner, son Jim.

Pressing business. Carmichael printer Leonard R. Willingham (right), shows sons Leonard and Scott proofs of this book. Granddaughter Alexandria has the cover. The father-and-sons company, Colors Printing and Graphics, has operated in Carmichael since 1989.

Above: Rosemary and Gordon Martell's roadside store, The Farmer's Wife, has been a Carmichael institution for over 30 years. The couple's daughter Jeanette (back center), daily commutes 60 miles to help in the store.

Left: exhausted by the pre-Sabbath rush, kosher deli owner Bob Gittleman has a quick loaf with his baker wife Shira. As the only glatt-kosher deli in Sacramento, Bob's Butcher Block attracts purists from all over the county. Daughter Millie waits on her parents.

Chapanian children and grandkids (above), grew up in one of Carmichael's oldest continuous businesses. In 1978, Ron and Pearl Chapanian (seated right), bought a Fair Oaks Blvd store that had sold furniture since before WW2. Daughters Pam and Trish learned the business, as did grandaughter Torie (center). Coffee table cherub is grandaughter Ronnie, already a dab hand with the yardstick.

It takes three to tango. Arthur Murrray ballroom studio owners Frank Williams and wife Lisa (above), take baby daughter Lioness dancing with the stars in Carmichael.

Right: Dave Kovar (second from left), founded a Carmichael martial arts business that went national. Three generations of his fighting-fit family strut their martial stuff on the Fair Oaks Blvd bend known as Kovar's Corner. Kovar's brother Tim, (left), is C.E.O. Daughter Melissa (in white), had her karate brown belt at eight.

Eccentricities of Carmichael...

Yes, Carmichael folk sometimes demonstrate different hitches to their gitalongs...

Right: businessman George Holmes airs an offbeat humor on his Fair Oaks Blvd store marquee.

Early developers planned a sidewalk-free Carmichael ostensibly to preserve the rural nature of the area. In truth, such a policy saved them a fortune. Below: pupils of the Hidden Treasure Nursery take a supervised morning walk.

89

Staff and clients at
Fat Cat Tattoo have
Americana under and
over their skin.

Above: living opposite the Department of Motor Vehicles does not faze vintage car buff Rick Mitchell. His 1927 Dodge Tourig - complete with hickory spokes - has never failed a mechanical test.

Beside a Fair Oaks Blvd dental building, a teenage punk rocker (above left), reflects on his retro image.

Below left: Gregg and Ginny Gregory pause for a tipple in the "Lion's Head," an English pub they created in their 1920s Carmichael home.

Below: Snow White would be welcome in this garden.

Neighboring a millionaire's mansion, this Carmichael garden lacks no convenience.

Above: "this old dollhouse," says a Carmichael mom "shows my grown-up daughter she can always come home."

Railway enthusiast Bill Reece built his "Skunk Creek" miniature railroad around his (and neighbors') Carmichael properties. Though this dedicated engineer has passed on, his wife Joyce (seated right), still enjoys sharing the eccentric plaything with family and friends.

Comfortably rooted in the trunk
of a 90-year-old California Ave
palm, this fig tree phenomenon
has been featured in National
Geographic Magazine.

Artists/Artistes

Sculptor Kurt Runstadler (left), whose patrons have included Oprah Winfrey and composer Quincy Jones, farewells a batch of creations from his Carmichael studio. In the vanguard, one figure exhibits separation anxiety.

Below: actress Linda Small prepares for a performance at Carmichael's Chautauqua Playhouse, La Sierra Community Center. The intimate theatre provides a full season of comedies, dramas, musicals and children's productions.

Artist Denna Pro (above), lets one of her favorite paintings hog the limelight during a retrospective exhibition of her work at the Carmichael Presbyterian Church.

Below: Jerry Lopes conducts the Capitol Pops Concert Band in the Danny Bishop Memorial Music Shell, Carmichael Park. Free summer concerts are a highlight of community life.

Above: Carmichael pianist and composer Dr Joe Gilman gives a concert in a private home. Internationally acclaimed, the jazz virtuoso has worked with Mel Tormé and Dave Brubeck. Carmichael guitarist Steve Homan is a frequent partner in jazz .

Left: artists sketch from life at the Sacramento Fine Arts Center, Gibbons Dr.

Choreographed for four prima danseuses in the 1840s, the ballet Pas de Quartre is restaged in a private garden. Carmichael ballerina Hannah Blank (left), and friends Alison Woodruff, Brynn Vogel and Heather Hopkins study at the Capitol Ballet Company, Marconi Ave.

Above: internationally-collected painter Jian Wang often works in plein air at the Sarah Place river access, where water seems to pour from this large canvas. The American River, says Wang, "has influenced over half of my paintings."

Above: the Sacramento Fine Arts Center's painted umbrella festival (Shades of Carmichael) provides a shady place for sunny people in Carmichael Park.

Left: Pat Mahony's landscape and still-life studies are avidly collected. In the painter's Carmichael studio, toy terrier Little Eva provides a welcome distraction.

Jewels in the Crown...
Ancil Hoffman Park

Fog and frost chill a winter morning.

Ancil Hoffman Park extends the American River Parkway through Carmichael.
Its golf course is as popular for wildlife as it is for humans.

Above: on horse trails around the park golf course, an equestrian cuts a romantic figure.

Different spokes for different folks. School friends (right), exercise in the park's open spaces.

Below: at dusk, an egret awaits a winter dinner.

Including undeveloped reserves, Carmichael Parks and Recreation District administers 13 parks. A lesser-known gem is the Charles C. Jensen Botanical Gardens on Fair Oaks Blvd.

Below: at the Harrington Ave access to the American River Parkway, playful retrievers find the water too delicious to resist.

Party hearty. Seniors dance (above), at the Mission Oaks Community Center, Gibbons Dr. The facility is a busy hub for recreation, education and senior events.

Above: the most canine-friendly reserve in Sacramento County, Carmichael Park has areas where dogs can socialise and run off-leash. Small dog owners (above), lobbied successfuly for a separate corral for petits pooches.

Left: Santa Claus greets fans at Carmichael Park Christmas festivities. Hosts are Carmichael Parks and Recreation Board members Bonnie Berns and Jerry Dover.

And More Jewels...

Mary and Claude Capra established Capra Park as a horse ranch in the early 1940s. It was a frequent vacation spot for their relative, moviemaker Frank Capra. After her husband's death, Mary Capra bequeathed the land to the Carmichael community. Carmichael Parks and Recreation administers the Kenneth Ave reserve. Left: filly Mya admires a plaque honoring her benefactors.

Below: locally known as "Little Africa," Schweitzer Grove Nature Area (near Stollwood Dr.), is a 17-acre eucalyptus forest and home to a disk golf course. See more on this sport, page 59.

Pond at the Pond. Father of the American River Parkway, William C. Pond gave his name to one of Carmichael's most beloved parks. Sacramento's first head of Parks and Recreation in the 1960s, he masterminded the formation of 30 miles of riverside reserves that are the County's most treasured recreational asset. Above: marking 66 years of marriage, Pond and wife Louise are greeted by Canada geese at William C. Pond Park.

Our Last Pictures Show...

Some of the Carmichael our grandparents recall still exists-for now.
Let's treasure our remnants of unabashed Americana

Right: Mom Jody Wheaton (in apron), runs the local 4-H Club. Formed in the early 1900s, the national organization extolls rural children to develop Head, Heart, Hands and Health. Carmichael members include the Wheaton kids, whose bunnies hop off with prizes from the annual Sacramento County Fair.

Below: Norman Rockwell's famous farmyard painting is restaged by Susan Maxwell Skinner, as "a vignette for local history books." Kneeling is long-serving Carmichael vet Major Nilson. Asks the photographer: "Who knows how much longer there will be family farmlets in Carmichael? I hope shots like this help to immortalize an under-appreciated national treasure: the small American town."